FAVORITE BRAND NAME™

Duncan Hines®

Publications International, Ltd.

Favorite Brand Name Recipes at www.fbnr.com

Photographs on pages 6, 15, 21, 30, 41, 63, 85 and 121 © Publications International, Ltd. All other photographs © Aurora Foods Inc.

Favorite Brand Name is a trademark of Publications International, Ltd.

Duncan Hines® and Moist Deluxe® are registered trademarks of Aurora Foods Inc.

Pictured on the front cover: Carrot Layer Cake *(page 78).*
Pictured on the back cover: Hot Fudge Sundae Cake *(page 116).*

ISBN: 1-4127-2264-0

Manufactured in China.

8 7 6 5 4 3 2 1

Microwave Cooking: Microwave ovens vary in wattage. Use the cooking times as guidelines and check for doneness before adding more time.

Table of Contents

Chocolate Obsession

Nothing is more sensuous or satisfying than chocolate. Go ahead and indulge your cravings with this incredible assortment of treats from tortes to truffles. Duncan Hines® makes luscious chocolate desserts a piece of cake.

Chocolate Peanut Butter Cups

1 package DUNCAN HINES® Moist Deluxe® Swiss Chocolate
   Cake Mix
1 container DUNCAN HINES® Creamy Home-Style Classic
   Vanilla Frosting
$^{1}/_{2}$ cup creamy peanut butter
15 miniature peanut butter cup candies, wrappers removed, cut in
   half vertically

1. Preheat oven to 350°F. Place 30 (2$^{1}/_{2}$-inch) paper liners in muffin
cups.

2. Prepare, bake and cool cupcakes following package directions for basic
recipe.

3. Combine vanilla frosting and peanut butter in medium bowl. Stir until
smooth. Frost one cupcake. Decorate with peanut butter cup candy, cut
side down. Repeat with remaining cupcakes, frosting and candies.

Makes 30 servings

Tip: You may substitute Duncan Hines® Moist Deluxe® Devil's Food, Dark
Chocolate Fudge or Butter Recipe Fudge Cake Mix flavors for Swiss
Chocolate Cake Mix.

Upside-Down German Chocolate Cake

1 $^1/_2$ cups flaked coconut

1 $^1/_2$ cups chopped pecans

1 package DUNCAN HINES® Moist Deluxe® German Chocolate or Classic Chocolate Cake Mix

1 package (8 ounces) cream cheese, softened

$^1/_2$ cup butter or margarine, melted

1 pound (3$^1/_2$ to 4 cups) confectioners' sugar

1. Preheat oven to 350°F. Grease and flour 13×9-inch pan.

2. Spread coconut evenly on bottom of prepared pan. Sprinkle with pecans. Prepare cake mix as directed on package. Pour over coconut and pecans. Combine cream cheese and melted butter in medium mixing bowl. Beat at low speed with electric mixer until creamy. Add sugar; beat until blended and smooth. Drop by spoonfuls evenly over cake batter. Bake at 350°F for 45 to 50 minutes or until toothpick inserted halfway to bottom of cake comes out clean. Cool completely in pan. To serve, cut into individual pieces; turn upside down onto plate.

Makes 12 to 16 servings

Tip: This cake can be served warm, if desired. Also, store leftover coconut in the refrigerator and use within four weeks.

Upside-Down German Chocolate Cake

Chocolate Cherry Torte

1 package DUNCAN HINES® Moist Deluxe® Devil's Food
Cake Mix
1 can (21 ounces) cherry pie filling
¼ teaspoon almond extract
1 container (8 ounces) frozen whipped topping, thawed and
divided
¼ cup toasted sliced almonds, for garnish (see Tip)

1. Preheat oven to 350°F. Grease and flour two 9-inch round cake pans.

2. Prepare, bake and cool cake following package directions for basic recipe. Combine cherry pie filling and almond extract in small bowl. Stir until blended.

3. To assemble, place one cake layer on serving plate. Spread with 1 cup whipped topping, then half the cherry pie filling mixture. Top with second cake layer. Spread remaining pie filling to within 1½ inches of cake edge. Decorate cake edge with remaining whipped topping. Garnish with sliced almonds.   *Makes 12 to 16 servings*

Tip: To toast almonds, spread in a single layer on baking sheet. Bake at 325°F 4 to 6 minutes or until fragrant and golden.

Chocolate Cherry Torte

Chocolate Streusel Cake

STREUSEL

    1 package DUNCAN HINES® Moist Deluxe® Devil's Food
       Cake Mix, divided

    1 cup finely chopped pecans

    2 tablespoons brown sugar

    2 teaspoons ground cinnamon

CAKE

    3 eggs

  1 1/3 cups water

   1/2 cup vegetable oil

TOPPING

    1 container (8 ounces) frozen whipped topping, thawed

    3 tablespoons sifted unsweetened cocoa powder

    Chopped pecans for garnish (optional)

    Chocolate curls for garnish (optional)

1. Preheat oven to 350°F. Grease and flour 10-inch Bundt pan.

2. For streusel, combine 2 tablespoons cake mix, 1 cup pecans, brown sugar and cinnamon. Set aside.

3. For cake, combine remaining cake mix, eggs, water and oil in large bowl. Beat at medium speed with electric mixer for 2 minutes. Pour two-thirds of batter into prepared pan. Sprinkle with reserved streusel. Pour remaining batter evenly over streusel. Bake at 350°F for 55 to 60 minutes or until toothpick inserted in center comes out clean. Cool in pan 25 minutes. Invert onto serving plate. Cool completely.

4. For topping, place whipped topping in medium bowl. Fold in cocoa until blended. Spread on cooled cake. Garnish with chopped pecans and chocolate curls, if desired. Refrigerate until ready to serve.

Makes 12 to 16 servings

Tip: For chocolate curls, warm chocolate in microwave oven at HIGH (100% power) for 5 to 10 seconds. Make chocolate curls by holding a sharp vegetable peeler against the flat side of a chocolate block and bringing the blade toward you. Apply firm pressure for thicker, more open curls or light pressure for tighter curls.

Chocolate Streusel Cake

Banana Fudge Layer Cake

1 package DUNCAN HINES® Moist Deluxe® Yellow Cake Mix
1⅓ cups water
3 eggs
⅓ cup vegetable oil
1 cup mashed ripe bananas (about 3 medium)
1 container DUNCAN HINES® Chocolate Frosting

1. Preheat oven to 350°F. Grease and flour two 9-inch round cake pans.

2. Combine cake mix, water, eggs and oil in large bowl. Beat at low speed with electric mixer until moistened. Beat at medium speed 2 minutes. Stir in bananas.

3. Pour into prepared pans. Bake at 350°F for 28 to 31 minutes or until toothpick inserted in center comes out clean. Cool in pans 15 minutes. Remove from pans; cool completely.

4. Fill and frost cake with frosting. Garnish as desired.

Makes 12 to 16 servings

Banana Fudge Layer Cake

Chocolate Almond Confection Cake

CAKE

    1 package (7 ounces) pure almond paste

    $1/2$ cup vegetable oil, divided plus additional for greasing

    3 eggs

    1 package DUNCAN HINES® Moist Deluxe® Devil's Food
        Cake Mix

  $1 1/3$ cups water

GLAZE

    1 package (6 ounces) semisweet chocolate chips

    3 tablespoons cherry jelly or seedless red raspberry jam

    2 tablespoons butter or margarine

    1 tablespoon light corn syrup

      Natural sliced almonds, for garnish

      Candied whole maraschino cherries or fresh raspberries,
        for garnish

1. Preheat oven to 350°F. Grease and flour 10-inch Bundt or tube pan.

2. For cake, combine almond paste and 2 tablespoons oil in large bowl. Beat at medium speed with electric mixer until blended. Add remaining oil, 2 tablespoons at a time, until blended. Add 1 egg; beat at medium speed until blended. Add remaining 2 eggs; beat until smooth. Add cake mix and water; beat at medium speed for 2 minutes. Pour into pan. Bake at 350°F for 50 to 55 minutes or until toothpick inserted in center comes out clean. Cool in pan 25 minutes. Invert onto cooling rack. Cool completely.

3. For glaze, place chocolate chips, cherry jelly, butter and corn syrup in microwave-safe medium bowl. Microwave at HIGH (100% power) for 1 to 1½ minutes. Stir until melted and smooth. Glaze top of cake. Garnish with sliced almonds and maraschino cherries.

Makes 12 to 16 servings

Tip: This recipe may also be prepared in the food processor. Place almond paste in work bowl with knife blade. Process until finely chopped. Add cake mix, eggs, water and oil. Process for 1 minute or until smooth. Bake and cool as directed above.

Truffles

1 container DUNCAN HINES® Creamy Home-Style
    Milk Chocolate Frosting
2½ cups confectioners' sugar
1 cup pecan halves, divided
1 cup semisweet chocolate chips
3 tablespoons shortening

1. Combine frosting and sugar in large mixing bowl. Stir with wooden spoon until thoroughly blended. Chop ⅓ cup pecan halves; set aside. Cover remaining pecan halves with 1 tablespoon frosting mixture each.

2. Place chocolate chips and shortening in 2-cup glass measuring cup. Microwave at MEDIUM (50% power) for 2 minutes; stir. Microwave 1 minute at MEDIUM; stir until smooth. Dip one pecan ball into chocolate mixture until completely covered. Remove with fork to cooling rack. Sprinkle top with chopped pecans. Repeat until all candy balls are covered. Allow to stand until chocolate mixture is set.

Makes about 3 dozen candies

Double Chocolate Chewies

1 package DUNCAN HINES® Moist Deluxe® Butter Recipe
    Fudge Cake Mix

2 eggs

½ cup butter or margarine, melted

1 package (6 ounces) semisweet chocolate chips

1 cup chopped nuts

    Confectioners' sugar (optional)

1. Preheat oven to 350°F. Grease 13×9×2-inch pan.

2. Combine cake mix, eggs and melted butter in large bowl. Stir until thoroughly blended. (Mixture will be stiff.) Stir in chocolate chips and nuts. Press mixture evenly in prepared pan. Bake at 350°F for 25 to 30 minutes or until toothpick inserted in center comes out clean. *Do not overbake.* Cool completely. Cut into bars. Dust with confectioners' sugar, if desired.

Makes 36 bars

Tip: For a special effect, cut a paper towel into ¼-inch-wide strips. Place strips in diagonal pattern on top of cooled bars before cutting. Place confectioners' sugar in tea strainer. Tap strainer lightly to dust surface with sugar. Carefully remove strips.

Double Chocolate Chewies

Chocolate Chip Cheesecake

1 package DUNCAN HINES® Moist Deluxe® Devil's Food
    Cake Mix
$1/2$ cup vegetable oil
3 packages (8 ounces each) cream cheese, softened
$1 1/2$ cups granulated sugar
1 cup sour cream
$1 1/2$ teaspoons vanilla extract
4 eggs, lightly beaten
$3/4$ cup mini semisweet chocolate chips, divided
1 teaspoon all-purpose flour

1. Preheat oven to 350°F. Grease 10-inch springform pan.

2. Combine cake mix and oil in large bowl. Mix well. Press onto bottom of prepared pan. Bake at 350°F for 22 to 25 minutes or until set. Remove from oven. *Increase oven temperature to 450°F.*

3. Place cream cheese in large mixing bowl. Beat at low speed with electric mixer, adding sugar gradually. Add sour cream and vanilla extract, mixing until blended. Add eggs, mixing only until incorporated. Toss $1/2$ cup chocolate chips with flour. Fold into cream cheese mixture. Pour filling onto crust. Sprinkle with remaining $1/4$ cup chocolate chips. Bake at 450°F for 5 to 7 minutes. *Reduce oven temperature to 250°F.* Bake at 250°F for 60 to 65 minutes or until set. Loosen cake from side of pan with knife or spatula. Cool completely in pan on cooling rack. Refrigerate until ready to serve. Remove side of pan. *Makes 12 to 16 servings*

Tip: Place pan of water on bottom shelf of oven during baking to prevent cheesecake from cracking.

Chocolate Chip Cheesecake

Coconut Chocolate Chip Loaf

1 package DUNCAN HINES® Bakery-Style Chocolate Chip
    Muffin Mix

1 1/3 cups toasted flaked coconut (see Tip)

3/4 cup water

1 egg

1/2 teaspoon vanilla extract

Confectioners' sugar for garnish (optional)

1. Preheat oven to 350°F. Grease and flour 9×5×3-inch loaf pan.

2. Empty muffin mix into medium bowl. Break up any lumps. Add coconut, water, egg and vanilla extract. Stir until moistened, about 50 strokes. Pour into prepared pan. Bake at 350°F for 45 to 50 minutes or until toothpick inserted in center comes out clean. Cool in pan 15 minutes. Invert onto cooling rack. Turn right side up. Cool completely. Dust with confectioners' sugar, if desired.   *Makes 1 loaf (12 slices)*

Tip: Spread coconut evenly on baking sheet. Toast at 350°F for 5 minutes. Stir and toast 1 to 2 minutes longer or until light golden brown.

Coconut Chocolate Chip Loaf

Triple Chocolate Fantasy

CAKE

    1 package DUNCAN HINES® Moist Deluxe® Devil's Food
        Cake Mix

    3 eggs

1 1/3 cups water

  1/2 cup vegetable oil plus additional for greasing

  1/2 cup ground walnuts

CHOCOLATE GLAZE

    1 package (12 ounces) semisweet chocolate chips

  1/4 cup plus 2 tablespoons butter or margarine

  1/4 cup coarsely chopped walnuts

WHITE CHOCOLATE GLAZE

    3 ounces white chocolate, coarsely chopped

    1 tablespoon shortening

1. Preheat oven to 350°F. Grease and flour 10-inch Bundt pan.

2. For cake, combine cake mix, eggs, water, oil and ground walnuts in large bowl. Beat at medium speed with electric mixer for 2 minutes. Pour into prepared pan. Bake at 350°F for 45 to 55 minutes or until toothpick inserted in center comes out clean. Cool in pan 25 minutes. Invert onto serving plate. Cool completely.

3. For chocolate glaze, combine chocolate chips and butter in small heavy saucepan. Heat on low heat until chips are melted. Stir constantly until shiny and smooth. (Glaze will be very thick.) Spread hot glaze over cooled cake. Sprinkle with coarsely chopped walnuts.

4. For white chocolate glaze, combine white chocolate and shortening in small heavy saucepan. Heat on low heat until melted, stirring constantly. Drizzle hot glaze over top and sides of cake. *Makes 12 to 16 servings*

Cindy's Fudgy Brownies

1 (21-ounce) package DUNCAN HINES® Family-Style Chewy
    Fudge Brownie Mix
1 egg
$^1\!/_3$ cup water
$^1\!/_3$ cup vegetable oil
$^3\!/_4$ cup semisweet chocolate chips
$^1\!/_2$ cup chopped pecans

1. Preheat oven to 350°F. Grease bottom only of 13×9×2-inch pan.

2. Combine brownie mix, egg, water and oil in large bowl. Stir with spoon until well blended, about 50 strokes. Stir in chocolate chips. Spread in prepared pan. Sprinkle with pecans. Bake at 350°F for 25 to 28 minutes or until set. Cool completely. Cut into bars. *Makes 24 brownies*

Tip: Overbaking brownies will cause them to become dry. Follow the recommended baking times given in recipes closely.

Chocolate Toffee Crunch Fantasy

1 package DUNCAN HINES® Moist Deluxe® Devil's Food
    Cake Mix
12 bars (1.4 ounces each) chocolate covered toffee bars, divided
  3 cups whipping cream, chilled

1. Preheat oven to 350°F. Grease and flour 10-inch tube pan.

2. Prepare, bake and cool cake following package directions. Split cake horizontally into three layers; set aside. Chop 11 candy bars into pea-size pieces (see Tip). Whip cream until stiff peaks form. Fold candy pieces into whipped cream.

3. To assemble, place one split cake layer on serving plate. Spread 1½ cups whipped cream mixture on top. Repeat with remaining layers and whipped cream mixture. Frost sides and top with remaining filling. Chop remaining candy bar coarsely. Sprinkle over top. Refrigerate until ready to serve.

Makes 12 servings

Tip: To quickly chop toffee candy bars, place a few bars in food processor fitted with steel blade. Pulse several times until pea-size pieces form. Repeat with remaining candy bars.

Chocolate Toffee Crunch Fantasy

Chocolate Cream Torte

1 package DUNCAN HINES® Moist Deluxe® Devil's Food
   Cake Mix
1 package (8 ounces) cream cheese, softened
½ cup sugar
1 teaspoon vanilla extract
1 cup finely chopped pecans
1 cup whipping cream, chilled
   Strawberry halves for garnish
   Mint leaves for garnish

1. Preheat oven to 350°F. Grease and flour two 8- or 9-inch round cake pans.

2. Prepare, bake and cool cake following package directions for basic recipe. Chill layers for ease in splitting.

3. Place cream cheese, sugar and vanilla extract in small bowl. Beat at low speed with electric mixer until smooth. Add pecans; stir until blended. Set aside. Beat whipping cream in small bowl until stiff peaks form. Fold whipped cream into cream cheese mixture.

4. To assemble, split each cake layer in half horizontally (see Tip). Place one cake layer on serving plate. Spread top with one fourth of filling. Repeat with remaining layers and filling. Garnish with strawberry halves and mint leaves, if desired. Refrigerate until ready to serve.

Makes 12 to 16 servings

Tip: To split layers evenly, measure cake with ruler. Divide into 2 equal layers. Mark with toothpicks. Cut through layers with serrated knife, using toothpicks as guide.

Chocolate Cream Torte

Collectible Cookies

Whether they're chewy or crisp, round or rectangular, cookies bring a smile to everyone's face. With Duncan Hines® mixes it's so easy to make the family's favorite treats, you may never have an empty cookie jar again.

Chocolate Oat Chewies

1 package DUNCAN HINES® Moist Deluxe® Devil's Food
   Cake Mix
1$^1/_3$ cups old-fashioned oats, uncooked
1 cup flaked coconut, toasted and divided
$^3/_4$ cup butter or margarine, melted
2 eggs, beaten
1 teaspoon vanilla extract
5 bars (1.55 ounces each) milk chocolate, cut into rectangles

1. Preheat oven to 350°F.

2. Combine cake mix, oats, $^1/_2$ cup coconut, butter, eggs and vanilla extract in large bowl. Cover and chill 15 minutes.

3. Shape dough into 1-inch balls. Place balls 2 inches apart on ungreased baking sheets. Bake at 350°F for 12 minutes or until tops are slightly cracked. Remove from oven. Press one milk chocolate rectangle into center of each cookie. Sprinkle with remaining $^1/_2$ cup coconut. Remove to cooling racks.

Makes about 4$^1/_2$ dozen cookies

Pinwheel Cookies

$^1/_2$ cup shortening plus additional for greasing
$^1/_3$ cup plus 1 tablespoon butter, softened and divided
2 egg yolks
$^1/_2$ teaspoon vanilla extract
1 package DUNCAN HINES® Moist Deluxe® Fudge Marble
    Cake Mix

1. Combine $^1/_2$ cup shortening, $^1/_3$ cup butter, egg yolks and vanilla extract in large bowl. Mix at low speed of electric mixer until blended. Set aside cocoa packet from cake mix. Gradually add cake mix. Blend well.

2. Divide dough in half. Add cocoa packet and remaining 1 tablespoon butter to one half of dough. Knead until well blended and chocolate colored.

3. Roll out yellow dough between two pieces of waxed paper into 18×12×1/8-inch rectangle. Repeat for chocolate dough. Remove top pieces of waxed paper from chocolate and yellow doughs. Place yellow dough directly on top of chocolate dough. Remove remaining layers of waxed paper. Roll up jelly-roll fashion, beginning at wide side. Refrigerate 2 hours.

4. Preheat oven to 350°F. Grease baking sheets.

5. Cut dough into $^1/_8$-inch slices. Place sliced dough 1 inch apart on prepared baking sheets. Bake at 350°F for 9 to 11 minutes or until lightly browned. Cool 5 minutes on baking sheets. Remove to cooling racks.   *Makes about 3$^1/_2$ dozen cookies*

Pinwheel Cookies

Cinnamon Stars

2 tablespoons sugar

¾ teaspoon ground cinnamon

¾ cup butter or margarine, softened

2 egg yolks

1 teaspoon vanilla extract

1 package DUNCAN HINES® Moist Deluxe® French Vanilla
Cake Mix

1. Preheat oven to 375°F. Combine sugar and cinnamon in small bowl. Set aside.

2. Combine butter, egg yolks and vanilla extract in large bowl. Blend in cake mix gradually. Roll dough to ⅛-inch thickness on lightly floured surface. Cut with 2½-inch star cookie cutter. Place 2 inches apart on ungreased baking sheet.

3. Sprinkle cookies with cinnamon-sugar mixture. Bake at 375°F for 6 to 8 minutes or until edges are light golden brown. Cool 1 minute on baking sheet. Remove to cooling rack. Cool completely. Store in airtight container.   *Makes 3 to 3½ dozen cookies*

Tip: You can use your favorite cookie cutter in place of the star cookie cutter.

Cinnamon Stars

Sweet Walnut Maple Bars

CRUST

    1 package DUNCAN HINES® Moist Deluxe® Classic Yellow
        Cake Mix, divided
    $1/3$ cup butter or margarine, melted
    1 egg

TOPPING

    $1\,1/3$ cups MRS. BUTTERWORTH'S® Maple Syrup
    3 eggs
    $1/3$ cup firmly packed light brown sugar
    $1/2$ teaspoon maple flavoring or vanilla extract
    1 cup chopped walnuts

1. Preheat oven to 350°F. Grease 13×9×2-inch pan.

2. For crust, reserve $2/3$ cup cake mix; set aside. Combine remaining cake mix, melted butter and egg in large bowl. Stir until thoroughly blended. (Mixture will be crumbly.) Press into prepared pan. Bake at 350°F for 15 to 20 minutes or until light golden brown.

3. For topping, combine reserved cake mix, maple syrup, eggs, brown sugar and maple flavoring in large bowl. Beat at low speed with electric mixer for 3 minutes. Pour over crust. Sprinkle with walnuts. Bake at 350°F for 30 to 35 minutes or until filling is set. Cool completely. Cut into bars. Store leftover cookie bars in refrigerator.   *Makes 24 bars*

Sweet Walnut Maple Bars

Chocolate Almond Biscotti

1 package DUNCAN HINES® Moist Deluxe® Dark Chocolate
  Cake Mix
1 cup all-purpose flour
$^1/_2$ cup butter or margarine, melted
2 eggs
1 teaspoon almond extract
$^1/_2$ cup chopped almonds
  White chocolate, melted (optional)

1. Preheat oven to 350°F. Line 2 baking sheets with parchment paper.

2. Combine cake mix, flour, butter, eggs and almond extract in large bowl.
Beat at low speed with electric mixer until well blended; stir in almonds.
Divide dough in half. Shape each half into 12×2-inch log; place logs on
prepared baking sheets. (Bake logs separately.)

3. Bake at 350°F for 30 to 35 minutes or until toothpick inserted in
centers comes out clean. Remove logs from oven; cool on baking sheets
15 minutes. Using serrated knife, cut logs into $^1/_2$-inch slices. Arrange
slices on baking sheets. Bake biscotti 10 minutes. Remove to cooling
racks; cool completely.

4. Dip one end of each biscotti in melted white chocolate, if desired.
Allow white chocolate to set at room temperature before storing biscotti in
airtight container.   *Makes about 2$^1/_2$ dozen cookies*

Chocolate Almond Biscotti

Fudgy Hazelnut Brownies

1 (21-ounce) package DUNCAN HINES® Chewy Fudge
   Brownie Mix
2 eggs
$^{1}/_{2}$ cup vegetable oil
$^{1}/_{4}$ cup water
1 cup chopped toasted hazelnuts
1 cup semisweet chocolate chips
1 cup DUNCAN HINES® Dark Chocolate Frosting
3 squares white chocolate, melted

1. Preheat oven to 350°F. Grease bottom only of 13×9-inch baking pan.

2. Combine brownie mix, eggs, oil and water in large bowl. Stir with spoon until well blended, about 50 strokes. Stir in hazelnuts and chocolate chips. Spread in prepared pan. Bake at 350°F for 25 to 30 minutes or until set. Cool completely.

3. Heat frosting in microwave oven at HIGH (100% power) for 15 seconds or until thin; stir well. Spread over brownies. Spoon dollops of white chocolate over chocolate frosting; marble white chocolate through frosting. Cool completely. Cut into bars.   *Makes 24 brownies*

Fudgy Hazelnut Brownies

Spicy Oatmeal Raisin Cookies

   1 package DUNCAN HINES® Moist Deluxe® Spice Cake Mix
   4 egg whites
   1 cup uncooked quick-cooking oats (not instant or old-fashioned)
  1/2 cup vegetable oil
  1/2 cup raisins

1. Preheat oven to 350°F. Grease baking sheets.

2. Combine cake mix, egg whites, oats and oil in large mixing bowl. Beat at low speed with electric mixer until blended. Stir in raisins. Drop by rounded teaspoonfuls onto prepared baking sheets.

3. Bake at 350°F for 7 to 9 minutes or until lightly browned. Cool 1 minute on baking sheets. Remove to cooling racks; cool completely.

Makes about 4 dozen cookies

Easy Lemon Cookies

   1 package DUNCAN HINES® Moist Deluxe® Lemon Cake Mix
   2 eggs
  1/2 cup vegetable oil
   1 teaspoon grated lemon peel
    Pecan halves for garnish

1. Preheat oven to 350°F.

2. Combine cake mix, eggs, oil and lemon peel in large bowl. Stir until thoroughly blended. Drop by rounded teaspoonfuls 2 inches apart onto ungreased baking sheets. Press pecan half into center of each cookie.

3. Bake at 350°F for 9 to 11 minutes or until edges are light golden brown. Cool 1 minute on baking sheets. Remove to wire racks. Cool completely. Store in airtight container.   *Makes 4 dozen cookies*

Tip: You can substitute whole almonds or walnut halves for the pecan halves.

Easy Lemon Cookies

Double Nut Chocolate Chip Cookies

1 package DUNCAN HINES® Moist Deluxe® Classic Yellow
    Cake Mix
$^{1}/_{2}$ cup butter or margarine, melted
1 egg
1 cup semisweet chocolate chips
$^{1}/_{2}$ cup finely chopped pecans
1 cup sliced almonds, divided

1. Preheat oven to 375°F. Grease baking sheets.

2. Combine cake mix, butter and egg in large bowl. Mix at low speed with electric mixer until just blended. Stir in chocolate chips, pecans and $^{1}/_{4}$ cup almonds. Shape rounded tablespoonfuls of dough into balls. Place remaining $^{3}/_{4}$ cup almonds in shallow bowl. Press tops of cookies into almonds. Place 1 inch apart on prepared baking sheets.

3. Bake at 375°F for 9 to 11 minutes or until lightly browned. Cool 2 minutes on baking sheets. Remove to cooling racks.

Makes 3 to 3$^{1}/_{2}$ dozen cookies

Double Nut Chocolate Chip Cookies

Coconut Clouds

2²/₃ cups flaked coconut, divided
1 package DUNCAN HINES® Moist Deluxe® Classic Yellow
  Cake Mix
1 egg
¹/₂ cup vegetable oil
¹/₄ cup water
1 teaspoon almond extract

1. Preheat oven to 350°F. Reserve 1¹/₃ cups coconut in medium bowl;
set aside.

2. Combine cake mix, egg, oil, water and almond extract in large bowl.
Beat at low speed with electric mixer. Stir in remaining 1¹/₃ cups coconut.
Drop rounded teaspoonfuls of dough into reserved coconut. Roll to cover
lightly. Place balls 2 inches apart on ungreased baking sheet. Repeat with
remaining dough. Bake at 350°F for 10 to 12 minutes or until light
golden brown. Cool 1 minute on baking sheets. Remove to cooling racks.
Cool completely. Store in airtight container.   *Makes 3¹/₂ dozen cookies*

Cook's Note: To save time when forming dough into balls, use a 1-inch
spring-operated cookie scoop. Spring-operated cookie scoops are available
at kitchen specialty shops.

Coconut Clouds

Double Mint Brownies

1 (21-ounce) package DUNCAN HINES® Family-Style Chewy
    Recipe Fudge Brownie Mix

1 egg

$^1/_3$ cup water

$^1/_3$ cup vegetable oil plus additional for greasing

$^1/_2$ teaspoon peppermint extract

24 chocolate-covered peppermint patties ($1^1/_2$ inches each)

1 cup confectioners' sugar, divided

4 teaspoons milk, divided

    Red food coloring

    Green food coloring

1. Preheat oven to 350°F. Grease bottom only of 13×9×2-inch pan. Combine brownie mix, egg, water, oil and peppermint extract in large bowl. Stir with spoon until well blended, about 50 strokes. Spread in prepared pan. Bake brownies following package directions. Place peppermint patties on warm brownies. Cool completely.

2. Combine $^1/_2$ cup confectioners' sugar, 2 teaspoons milk and 1 drop red food coloring in small bowl. Stir until smooth. Place in small resealable plastic bag; set aside. Repeat with remaining $^1/_2$ cup confectioners' sugar, remaining 2 teaspoons milk and 1 drop green food coloring. Cut pinpoint hole in bottom corner of each bag. Drizzle pink and green glazes over brownies as shown. Allow glazes to set before cutting into bars.

Makes 24 brownies

Tip: To prevent overdone edges and underdone center, wrap foil strips around outside edges of pan (do not cover bottom or top). Bake as directed above.

Double Mint Brownies

Orange Pecan Gems

1 package DUNCAN HINES® Moist Deluxe® Orange Supreme
   Cake Mix
1 container (8 ounces) vanilla low fat yogurt
1 egg
2 tablespoons butter or margarine, softened
1 cup finely chopped pecans
1 cup pecan halves

1. Preheat oven to 350°F. Grease baking sheets.

2. Combine cake mix, yogurt, egg, butter and chopped pecans in large
bowl. Beat at low speed with electric mixer until blended. Drop by rounded
teaspoonfuls 2 inches apart onto prepared baking sheets. Press pecan half
onto center of each cookie. Bake at 350°F for 11 to 13 minutes or until
golden brown. Cool 1 minute on baking sheets. Remove to cooling racks.
Cool completely. Store in airtight container.

Makes 4½ to 5 dozen cookies

Chocolate Peanut Butter Cookies

1 package DUNCAN HINES® Moist Deluxe® Devil's Food
   Cake Mix
¾ cup crunchy peanut butter
2 eggs
2 tablespoons milk
1 cup candy-coated peanut butter pieces

1. Preheat oven to 350°F. Grease baking sheets.

2. Combine cake mix, peanut butter, eggs and milk in large mixing bowl. Beat at low speed with electric mixer until blended. Stir in peanut butter pieces.

3. Drop dough by slightly rounded tablespoonfuls onto prepared baking sheets. Bake 7 to 9 minutes or until lightly browned. Cool 2 minutes on baking sheets. Remove to cooling racks.

Makes about 3¹/₂ dozen cookies

Tip: You can use 1 cup peanut butter chips in place of candy-coated peanut butter pieces.

Chocolate Peanut Butter Cookies

Fruit Fantasies

Create magical combinations with Duncan Hines® and nature's sweetest gift—fruit. You'll find recipes for shortcake, upside-down cake, layer cake and much more in fruit flavors from very berry to cool key lime.

Double Berry Layer Cake

1 package DUNCAN HINES® Moist Deluxe® Strawberry Supreme Cake Mix

$^2/_3$ cup strawberry jam, divided

$2^1/_2$ cups fresh blueberries, rinsed, drained and divided

1 container (8 ounces) frozen whipped topping, thawed and divided

Fresh strawberry slices for garnish

1. Preheat oven to 350°F. Grease and flour two 9-inch round cake pans.

2. Prepare, bake and cool cake following package directions for basic recipe.

3. Place one cake layer on serving plate. Spread with $^1/_3$ cup strawberry jam. Arrange 1 cup blueberries on jam. Spread half the whipped topping to within $^1/_2$ inch of cake edge. Place second cake layer on top. Repeat with remaining $^1/_3$ cup strawberry jam, 1 cup blueberries and remaining whipped topping. Garnish with strawberry slices and remaining $^1/_2$ cup blueberries. Refrigerate until ready to serve.   *Makes 12 servings*

Tip: For best results, cut cake with serrated knife; clean knife after each slice.

Blueberry Orange Muffins

1 package DUNCAN HINES® Bakery-Style Wild Maine
   Blueberry Muffin Mix
$^1/_2$ cup orange juice
2 egg whites
1 teaspoon grated orange peel

1. Preheat oven to 400°F. Grease $2^1/_2$-inch muffin cups (or use paper liners).

2. Rinse blueberries from Mix with cold water and drain.

3. Empty muffin mix into large bowl. Break up any lumps. Add orange juice, egg whites and orange peel. Stir until moistened, about 50 strokes. Fold blueberries gently into batter.

4. For large muffins, fill cups two-thirds full. Bake at 400°F for 18 to 21 minutes or until toothpick inserted into centers comes out clean. (For medium muffins, fill cups half full. Bake at 400°F for 16 to 19 minutes or until toothpick inserted into centers comes out clean.) Cool in pan 5 to 10 minutes. Carefully loosen muffins from pan. Remove to cooling racks. Serve warm or cool completely.   *Makes 8 large or 12 medium muffins*

Tip: Freeze extra grated orange peel for future use.

Peachy Cinnamon Coffeecake

1 can ($8^1/_4$ ounces) juice packed sliced yellow cling peaches
1 package DUNCAN HINES® Bakery-Style Cinnamon Swirl
   Muffin Mix
1 egg

1. Preheat oven to 400°F. Grease 8-inch square or 9-inch round pan.

2. Drain peaches, reserving juice. Add water to reserved juice to equal ¾ cup liquid. Chop peaches.

3. Combine muffin mix, egg and ¾ cup peach liquid in medium bowl; fold in peaches. Pour batter into prepared pan. Knead swirl packet 10 seconds before opening. Squeeze contents onto top of batter and swirl with knife. Sprinkle topping over batter. Bake at 400°F for 28 to 33 minutes for 8-inch pan (or 20 to 25 minutes for 9-inch pan) or until golden. Serve warm. *Makes 9 servings*

Peachy Cinnamon Coffeecake

Butter Pecan Banana Cake

CAKE

    1 package DUNCAN HINES® Moist Deluxe® Butter Recipe
       Golden Cake Mix

    4 eggs

    1 cup mashed ripe bananas (about 3 medium)

    ³/₄ cup vegetable oil

    ¹/₂ cup granulated sugar

    ¹/₄ cup milk

    1 teaspoon vanilla extract

    1 cup chopped pecans

FROSTING

    1 cup coarsely chopped pecans

    ¹/₄ cup butter or margarine

    1 container DUNCAN HINES® Vanilla Frosting

1. Preheat oven to 325°F. Grease and flour 10-inch Bundt or tube pan.

2. For cake, combine cake mix, eggs, bananas, oil, sugar, milk and vanilla extract in large mixing bowl. Beat at low speed with electric mixer until moistened. Beat at medium speed for 2 minutes. Stir in 1 cup chopped pecans. Pour into prepared pan. Bake 50 to 60 minutes or until toothpick inserted in center comes out clean. Cool in pan 25 minutes. Invert onto cooling rack. Cool completely.

3. For frosting, place 1 cup coarsely chopped pecans and butter in skillet. Cook on medium heat, stirring until pecans are toasted. Combine nut mixture and frosting in small bowl. Cool until spreading consistency. Frost cake.
Makes 12 to 16 servings

Butter Pecan Banana Cake

Luscious Key Lime Cake

CAKE

    1 package DUNCAN HINES® Moist Deluxe® Lemon Supreme
        Cake Mix

    1 package (4-serving size) lemon instant pudding and pie
        filling mix

    4 eggs

    1 cup vegetable oil

    $3/4$ cup water

    $1/4$ cup Key lime juice (see Tip)

GLAZE

    2 cups confectioners' sugar

    $1/3$ cup Key lime juice

    2 tablespoons water

    2 tablespoons butter or margarine, melted

        Additional confectioners' sugar

        Lime slices for garnish

        Fresh strawberry slices for garnish (optional)

1. Preheat oven to 350°F. Grease and flour 10-inch Bundt or tube pan.

2. For cake, combine cake mix, pudding mix, eggs, oil, $3/4$ cup water and $1/4$ cup Key lime juice in large bowl. Beat at low speed with electric mixer until moistened. Beat at medium speed 2 minutes. Pour into pan. Bake at 350°F 50 to 60 minutes or until toothpick inserted in center comes out clean. Cool in pan 25 minutes. Remove cake from pan onto cooling rack. Return cake to pan. Poke holes in top of warm cake with toothpick or long-tined fork.

3. For glaze, combine 2 cups confectioners' sugar, $\frac{1}{3}$ cup Key lime juice, 2 tablespoons water and melted butter in medium bowl. Pour slowly over top of warm cake. Cool completely. Invert onto serving plate. Dust with additional confectioners' sugar. Garnish with lime slices and strawberry slices, if desired.   *Makes 12 to 16 servings*

Tip: Fresh or bottled lime juice may be substituted for the Key lime juice.

Cranberry Cobbler

2 cans (16 ounces each) sliced peaches in light syrup, drained
1 can (16 ounces) whole berry cranberry sauce
1 package DUNCAN HINES® Cinnamon Swirl Muffin Mix
$\frac{1}{2}$ cup chopped pecans
$\frac{1}{3}$ cup butter or margarine, melted
    Whipped topping or ice cream

1. Preheat oven to 350°F.

2. Cut peach slices in half lengthwise. Combine peach slices and cranberry sauce in *ungreased* 9-inch square pan. Knead swirl packet from Mix for 10 seconds. Squeeze contents evenly over fruit.

3. Combine muffin mix, contents of topping packet from Mix and pecans in large bowl. Add melted butter. Stir until thoroughly blended (mixture will be crumbly). Sprinkle crumb mixture over fruit. Bake 40 to 45 minutes or until lightly browned and bubbly. Serve warm with whipped topping.   *Makes 9 servings*

Tip: Store leftovers in the refrigerator. Reheat in microwave oven to serve warm.

Strawberry Shortcake

CAKE

    1 package DUNCAN HINES® Moist Deluxe® French Vanilla
        Cake Mix

    3 eggs

 1 1/4 cups water

  1/2 cup butter or margarine, softened

FILLING AND TOPPING

    2 cups whipping cream, chilled

 1/3 cup sugar

 1/2 teaspoon vanilla extract

    1 quart fresh strawberries, rinsed, drained and sliced
    Mint leaves for garnish

1. Preheat oven to 350°F. Grease two 9-inch round cake pans with butter
or margarine. Sprinkle bottom and sides with granulated sugar.

2. For cake, combine cake mix, eggs, water and butter in large bowl. Beat
at low speed with electric mixer until moistened. Beat at medium speed for
2 minutes. Pour into prepared pans. Bake at 350°F for 30 to 35 minutes
or until toothpick inserted in center comes out clean. Cool in pan
10 minutes. Invert onto cooling rack. Cool completely.

3. For filling and topping, place whipping cream, sugar and vanilla extract in large bowl. Beat with electric mixer on high speed until stiff peaks form. Reserve $1/3$ cup for garnish. Place one cake layer on serving plate. Spread with half of whipped cream and half of sliced strawberries. Place second layer on top of strawberries. Spread with remaining whipping cream and top with remaining strawberries. Dollop with reserved $1/2$ cup whipped cream and garnish with mint leaves. Refrigerate until ready to serve. *Makes 12 servings*

Strawberry Shortcake

Lemon Bars

1 package DUNCAN HINES® Moist Deluxe® Lemon Supreme
   Cake Mix

3 eggs, divided

⅓ cup butter-flavor shortening

½ cup granulated sugar

¼ cup lemon juice

2 teaspoons grated lemon peel

½ teaspoon baking powder

¼ teaspoon salt

   Confectioners' sugar

1. Preheat oven to 350°F.

2. Combine cake mix, 1 egg and shortening in large mixing bowl. Beat at low speed with electric mixer until crumbs form. Reserve 1 cup. Pat remaining mixture lightly into *ungreased* 13×9-inch pan. Bake at 350°F for 15 minutes or until lightly browned.

3. Combine remaining 2 eggs, granulated sugar, lemon juice, lemon peel, baking powder and salt in medium mixing bowl. Beat at medium speed with electric mixer until light and foamy. Pour over hot crust. Sprinkle with reserved crumb mixture.

4. Bake at 350°F for 15 minutes or until lightly browned. Sprinkle with confectioners' sugar. Cool in pan. Cut into bars.   *Makes 30 to 32 bars*

Tip: These bars are also delicious using Duncan Hines® Moist Deluxe® Classic Yellow Cake Mix.

Lemon Bars

Pineapple Upside-Down Cake

TOPPING

$^1/_2$ cup butter or margarine

1 cup firmly packed brown sugar

1 can (20 ounces) pineapple slices, well drained

Maraschino cherries, drained and halved

Walnut halves

CAKE

1 package DUNCAN HINES® Moist Deluxe® Pineapple Supreme
Cake Mix

1 package (4-serving size) vanilla-flavor instant pudding and
pie filling mix

4 eggs

1 cup water

$^1/_2$ cup oil

1. Preheat oven to 350°F.

2. For topping, melt butter over low heat in 12-inch cast-iron skillet or skillet with oven-proof handle. Remove from heat. Stir in brown sugar. Spread to cover bottom of skillet. Arrange pineapple slices, maraschino cherries and walnut halves in skillet. Set aside.

3. For cake, combine cake mix, pudding mix, eggs, water and oil in large mixing bowl. Beat at medium speed with electric mixer for 2 minutes. Pour batter evenly over fruit in skillet. Bake at 350°F for 1 hour or until toothpick inserted in center comes out clean. Invert onto serving plate.

Makes 12 to 16 servings

Tip: Cake can be made in a 13×9×2-inch pan. Bake at 350°F for 45 to 55 minutes or until toothpick inserted in center comes out clean. Cake is also delicious using Duncan Hines® Moist Deluxe® Yellow Cake Mix.

Pineapple Upside Down Cake

Orange Cinnamon Swirl Bread

BREAD

> 1 package DUNCAN HINES® Bakery-Style Cinnamon Swirl
> Muffin Mix
>
> 1 egg
>
> $^2/_3$ cup orange juice
>
> 1 tablespoon grated orange peel

ORANGE GLAZE

> $^1/_2$ cup confectioners' sugar
>
> 2 to 3 teaspoons orange juice
>
> 1 teaspoon grated orange peel
>
> Quartered orange slices for garnish (optional)

1. Preheat oven to 350°F. Grease and flour 8$^1/_2$×4$^1/_2$×2$^1/_2$-inch loaf pan.

2. For bread, combine muffin mix and contents of topping packet from mix in large bowl. Break up any lumps. Add egg, $^2/_3$ cup orange juice and 1 tablespoon orange peel. Stir until moistened, about 50 strokes. Knead swirl packet from mix for 10 seconds before opening. Squeeze contents on top of batter. Swirl into batter with knife or spatula, folding from bottom of bowl to get an even swirl. *Do not completely mix in.* Pour into prepared pan. Bake at 350°F for 55 to 60 minutes or until toothpick inserted in center comes out clean. Cool in pan 10 minutes. Loosen loaf from pan. Invert onto cooling rack. Turn right side up. Cool completely.

3. For orange glaze, place confectioners' sugar in small bowl. Add orange juice, 1 teaspoon at a time, stirring until smooth and of desired consistency. Stir in 1 teaspoon orange peel. Drizzle over loaf. Garnish with orange slices, if desired. *Makes 1 loaf (12 slices)*

Orange Cinnamon Swirl Bread

Blueberry Cheesecake Bars

1 package DUNCAN HINES® Bakery-Style Blueberry Streusel
    Muffin Mix
$1/4$ cup cold butter or margarine
$1/3$ cup finely chopped pecans
1 package (8 ounces) cream cheese, softened
$1/2$ cup sugar
1 egg
3 tablespoons lemon juice
1 teaspoon grated lemon peel

1. Preheat oven to 350°F. Grease 9-inch square baking pan.

2. Rinse blueberries from Mix with cold water and drain; set aside.

3. Place muffin mix in medium bowl; cut in butter with pastry blender or two knives. Stir in pecans. Press into bottom of prepared pan. Bake at 350°F for 15 minutes or until set.

4. Combine cream cheese and sugar in medium bowl. Beat until smooth. Add egg, lemon juice and lemon peel. Beat well. Spread over baked crust. Sprinkle with blueberries. Sprinkle topping packet from Mix over blueberries. Return to oven. Bake at 350°F for 35 to 40 minutes or until filling is set. Cool completely. Refrigerate until ready to serve. Cut into bars.
Makes about 16 bars

Strawberry Stripe Refrigerator Cake

CAKE

    1 package DUNCAN HINES® Moist Deluxe® Classic White
        Cake Mix

    2 packages (10 ounces) frozen sweetened strawberry slices, thawed

TOPPING

    1 package (4-serving size) vanilla-flavor instant pudding and pie
        filling mix

    1 cup milk

    1 cup whipping cream, whipped

    Fresh strawberries for garnish (optional)

1. Preheat oven to 350°F. Grease and flour 13×9×2-inch pan.

2. For cake, prepare, bake and cool following package directions. Poke holes 1 inch apart in top of cake using handle of wooden spoon. Purée thawed strawberries with juice in blender or food processor. Spoon evenly over top of cake, allowing mixture to soak into holes.

3. For topping, combine pudding mix and milk in large bowl. Stir until smooth. Fold in whipped cream. Spread over cake. Decorate with fresh strawberries, if desired. Refrigerate at least 4 hours.

Makes 12 to 16 servings

Tip: For a Neapolitan Refrigerator Cake, replace the White Cake Mix with Duncan Hines® Moist Deluxe® Devil's Food Cake Mix and follow directions listed above.

Chocolate Banana Cake

CAKE

    1 package DUNCAN HINES® Moist Deluxe® Devil's Food
        Cake Mix

    3 eggs

  1 $1/3$ cups milk

   $1/2$ cup vegetable oil

TOPPING

    1 package (4-serving size) banana cream instant pudding and
        pie filling mix

    1 cup milk

    1 cup whipping cream, whipped

    1 medium banana

     Lemon juice

     Chocolate sprinkles for garnish

1. Preheat oven to 350°F. Grease and flour 13×9×2-inch pan.

2. For cake, combine cake mix, eggs, milk and oil in large bowl. Beat at low speed with electric mixer until moistened. Beat at medium speed 2 minutes. Pour into pan. Bake at 350°F 35 to 38 minutes or until toothpick inserted in center comes out clean. Cool completely.

3. For topping, combine pudding mix and milk in large bowl. Stir until smooth. Fold in whipped cream. Spread on top of cooled cake. Slice banana; dip in lemon juice, arrange on top. Garnish with chocolate sprinkles. Refrigerate until ready to serve.   *Makes 12 to 16 servings*

Tip: A wire whisk is a great utensil to use when making instant pudding. It quickly eliminates all lumps.

Chocolate Banana Cake

Berry Filled Muffins

1 package DUNCAN HINES® Bakery-Style Wild Maine
    Blueberry Muffin Mix

1 egg

$^1/_2$ cup water

$^1/_4$ cup strawberry jam

2 tablespoons sliced natural almonds

1. Preheat oven to 400°F. Place 8 (2$^1/_2$-inch) paper or foil liners in muffin cups; set aside.

2. Rinse blueberries from Mix with cold water and drain.

3. Empty muffin mix into bowl. Break up any lumps. Add egg and water. Stir until moistened, about 50 strokes. Fill cups half full with batter.

4. Fold blueberries into jam. Spoon on top of batter in each cup. Spread gently. Cover with remaining batter. Sprinkle with almonds. Bake at 400°F for 17 to 20 minutes or until set and golden brown. Cool in pan 5 to 10 minutes. Loosen carefully before removing from pan.

Makes 8 muffins

Refreshing Lemon Cake

1 package DUNCAN HINES® Moist Deluxe® Butter Recipe
    Golden Cake Mix

1 container DUNCAN HINES® Creamy Home-Style Cream
    Cheese Frosting

$^3/_4$ cup purchased lemon curd

Lemon drop candies, crushed for garnish (optional)

1. Preheat oven to 375°F. Grease and flour two 8- or 9-inch round cake pans.

2. Prepare, bake and cool cake following package directions for basic recipe.

3. To assemble, place one cake layer on serving plate. Place ¼ cup Cream Cheese frosting in small resealable plastic bag. Snip off one corner. Pipe a bead of frosting on top of layer around outer edge. Fill remaining area with lemon curd. Top with second cake layer. Spread remaining frosting on sides and top of cake. Garnish top of cake with crushed lemon candies, if desired.   *Makes 12 to 16 servings*

Tip: You can substitute Duncan Hines® Vanilla or Vanilla Buttercream frosting for the Cream Cheese frosting, if desired.

Refreshing Lemon Cake

Banana-Coconut Crunch Cake

CAKE

 1 package DUNCAN HINES® Moist Deluxe® Banana Supreme
    Cake Mix
 1 package (4-serving size) banana-flavor instant pudding and pie
    filling mix
 1 can (16 ounces) fruit cocktail, in juices, undrained
 4 eggs
 1/4 cup vegetable oil
 1 cup flaked coconut
 1/2 cup chopped pecans
 1/2 cup firmly packed brown sugar

GLAZE

 3/4 cup granulated sugar
 1/2 cup butter or margarine
 1/2 cup evaporated milk
 1 1/3 cups flaked coconut

1. Preheat oven to 350°F. Grease and flour 13×9×2-inch pan.

2. For cake, combine cake mix, pudding mix, fruit cocktail, eggs and oil in large bowl. Beat at medium speed with electric mixer for 4 minutes. Stir in 1 cup coconut. Pour into prepared pan. Combine pecans and brown sugar in small bowl. Sprinkle over batter. Bake at 350°F for 45 to 50 minutes or until toothpick inserted in center comes out clean.

3. For glaze, combine granulated sugar, butter and evaporated milk in medium saucepan. Bring to a boil. Cook for 2 minutes, stirring occasionally. Remove from heat. Stir in 1 1/3 cups coconut. Pour over warm cake.   *Makes 12 to 16 servings*

Banana-Coconut Crunch Cake

Sweet Celebrations

Start with a Duncan Hines® mix and turn dessert into a memorable occasion. Wow guests with a Trifle Spectacular or treat them to a devilishly easy Chocolate Angel Food Dessert. These recipes promise an elegant ending to any meal.

Cappuccino Bon Bons

1 (21-ounce) package DUNCAN HINES® Family-Style Chewy
   Fudge Brownie Mix
2 eggs
$^1/_3$ cup water
$^1/_3$ cup vegetable oil
$1^1/_2$ tablespoons instant coffee
1 teaspoon ground cinnamon
   Whipped topping
   Cinnamon

1. Preheat oven to 350°F. Place 2-inch foil cupcake liners on cookie sheet.

2. Combine brownie mix, eggs, water, oil, instant coffee and cinnamon. Stir with spoon until well blended, about 50 strokes. Fill each cupcake liner with 1 measuring tablespoon batter. Bake 12 to 15 minutes or until wooden toothpick inserted in center comes out clean. Cool completely. Garnish with whipped topping and a dash of cinnamon. Refrigerate until ready to serve.   *Makes about 40 bon bons*

Tip: To make larger bon bons, use twelve $2^1/_2$-inch foil cupcake liners and fill with $^1/_4$ cup batter. Bake 28 to 30 minutes.

Carrot Layer Cake

CAKE

> 1 package DUNCAN HINES® Moist Deluxe® Classic Yellow
> Cake Mix
>
> 4 eggs
>
> 1/2 cup vegetable oil
>
> 3 cups grated carrots
>
> 1 cup finely chopped nuts
>
> 2 teaspoons ground cinnamon

CREAM CHEESE FROSTING

> 1 package (8 ounces) cream cheese, softened
>
> 1/4 cup butter or margarine, softened
>
> 2 teaspoons vanilla extract
>
> 4 cups confectioners' sugar

1. Preheat oven to 350°F. Grease and flour two 8- or 9-inch round baking pans.

2. For cake, combine cake mix, eggs, oil, carrots, nuts and cinnamon in large bowl. Beat at low speed with electric mixer until moistened. Beat at medium speed for 2 minutes. Pour into prepared pans. Bake at 350°F for 35 to 40 minutes or until toothpick inserted in centers comes out clean. Cool.

3. For cream cheese frosting, place cream cheese, butter and vanilla extract in large bowl. Beat at low speed until smooth and creamy. Add confectioners' sugar gradually, beating until smooth. Add more sugar to thicken, or milk or water to thin frosting, as needed. Fill and frost cooled cake. Garnish with whole pecans. *Makes 12 to 16 servings*

Carrot Layer Cake

Fantasy Angel Food Cake

1 package DUNCAN HINES® Angel Food Cake Mix
 Red and green food coloring
1 container DUNCAN HINES® Creamy Home-Style Cream
  Cheese Frosting

1. Preheat oven to 350°F.

2. Prepare cake following package directions. Divide batter into thirds and place in 3 different bowls. Add a few drops red food coloring to one. Add a few drops green food coloring to another. Stir each until well blended. Leave the third one plain. Spoon pink batter into ungreased 10-inch tube pan. Cover with white batter and top with green batter. Bake and cool following package directions.

3. To make cream cheese glaze, heat frosting in microwave at HIGH (100% power) 20 to 30 seconds. Do not overheat. Stir until smooth. Set aside ¼ cup warm glaze. Spoon remaining glaze on top and sides of cake to completely cover. Divide remaining glaze in half and place in 2 different bowls. Add a few drops red food coloring to one. Add a few drops green food coloring to the other. Stir each until well blended. Using a teaspoon, drizzle green glaze around edge of cake so it will run down sides. Repeat with pink glaze. *Makes 16 servings*

Tip: For marble cake, drop batter by spoonfuls, alternating colors frequently.

Fantasy Angel Food Cake

Strawberry Celebration Cake

1 package DUNCAN HINES® Moist Deluxe® Strawberry
    Supreme Cake Mix
1 cup strawberry preserves, heated
1 container DUNCAN HINES® Creamy Home-Style Cream
    Cheese Frosting
    Strawberry halves for garnish
    Mint leaves for garnish

1. Preheat oven to 350°F. Grease and flour 10-inch Bundt or tube pan.

2. Prepare, bake and cool cake following package directions for basic recipe.

3. Split cake horizontally into three even layers. Place bottom cake layer on serving plate. Spread with $1/2$ cup warm preserves. Repeat layering. Top with remaining cake layer. Frost cake with Cream Cheese frosting. Garnish with strawberry halves and mint leaves. Refrigerate until ready to serve. *Makes 12 to 16 servings*

Tip: For a delicious variation, substitute 1 cup seedless red raspberry jam for the strawberry preserves.

Blueberry Angel Food Cake Rolls

1 package DUNCAN HINES® Angel Food Cake Mix
$1/4$ cup confectioners' sugar plus additional for dusting
1 can (21 ounces) blueberry pie filling
    Mint leaves for garnish (optional)

1. Preheat oven to 350°F. Line two $15^{1}/_{2} \times 10^{1}/_{2} \times 1$-inch jelly-roll pans with aluminum foil.

2. Prepare cake mix as directed on package. Divide and spread evenly into prepared pans. Cut through batter with knife or spatula to remove large air bubbles. Bake at 350°F for 15 minutes or until set. Invert cakes at once onto clean, lint-free dishtowels dusted with sugar. Remove foil carefully. Roll up each cake with towel jelly-roll fashion, starting at short end. Cool completely.

3. Unroll cakes. Spread about 1 cup blueberry pie filling to within 1 inch of edges on each cake. Reroll and place seam-side down on serving plate. Dust with ¼ cup sugar. Garnish with mint leaves, if desired.

Makes 2 cakes (8 servings each)

Tip: For a variation in flavor, substitute cherry pie filling for the blueberry pie filling.

Blueberry Angel Food Cake Roll

Orange Glazed Pound Cake

1 package DUNCAN HINES® Moist Deluxe® Butter Recipe
  Golden Cake Mix

4 eggs

1 cup sour cream

1/3 cup vegetable oil

1/4 cup plus 1 to 2 tablespoons orange juice, divided

2 tablespoons grated orange peel

1 cup confectioners' sugar

1. Preheat oven to 375°F. Grease and flour 10-inch tube pan.

2. Combine cake mix, eggs, sour cream, oil, 1/4 cup orange juice and orange peel in large bowl. Beat at medium speed with electric mixer for 2 minutes. Pour into prepared pan. Bake at 375°F for 45 to 50 minutes or until toothpick inserted in center comes out clean. Cool in pan 25 minutes. Invert onto cooling rack. Cool completely.

3. Combine sugar and remaining 1 to 2 tablespoons orange juice in small bowl; stir until smooth. Drizzle over cake. Garnish as desired.

Makes 12 to 16 servings

Orange Glazed Pound Cake

Ribbon Cake

CAKE

1 package DUNCAN HINES® Moist Deluxe® Classic White
    Cake Mix

1/4 cup flaked coconut, chopped

1/4 cup natural pistachio nuts, finely chopped
    Green food coloring

1/4 cup maraschino cherries, drained, finely chopped
    Red food coloring

FILLING AND FROSTING

3 1/4 cups confectioners' sugar

1/2 cup shortening

1/3 cup water

1/4 cup powdered non-dairy creamer

1 1/2 teaspoons vanilla extract

1/4 teaspoon salt
    Green food coloring

1/2 cup natural pistachio nuts, finely chopped

3/4 cup cherry jam
    Whole maraschino cherries with stems for garnish
    Mint leaves for garnish

1. Preheat oven to 350°F. Grease and flour three 8-inch square pans.

2. For cake, prepare cake mix following package directions for basic recipe. Combine 1 3/4 cups batter and coconut in small bowl; set aside. Combine 1 3/4 cups batter, pistachio nuts and 5 drops green food coloring in small bowl; set aside. Combine remaining batter, 1/4 cup chopped maraschino cherries and 2 drops red food coloring. Pour batters into separate pans. Bake at 350°F for 18 minutes or until toothpick inserted in center comes out clean. Cool and trim edges of cake.

3. For filling and frosting, combine confectioners' sugar, shortening, water, non-dairy creamer, vanilla extract, salt and 5 drops green food coloring in large bowl. Beat for 3 minutes at medium speed with electric mixer. Beat for 5 minutes at high speed. Add more confectioners' sugar to thicken or water to thin as needed. Add remaining ½ cup pistachio nuts. Stir until blended.

4. To assemble, spread green and white cake layers with cherry jam. Stack layers. Top with pink layer. Frost sides and top of cake. Garnish with whole maraschino cherries and mint leaves. *Makes 12 to 16 servings*

Tip: To save time, use Duncan Hines® Creamy Homestyle Vanilla Frosting. Tint with several drops green food coloring.

Ribbon Cake

Chocolate Angel Food Dessert

　1 package DUNCAN HINES® Angel Food Cake Mix
16 large marshmallows
$^1/_2$ cup milk
　1 package (11 ounces) milk chocolate chips
　2 cups whipping cream
$^1/_4$ cup semisweet chocolate chips
1 $^1/_2$ teaspoons shortening

1. Preheat oven to 375°F. Prepare, bake and cool cake following package directions.

2. Melt marshmallows and milk in heavy saucepan over low heat. Remove from heat; stir in milk chocolate chips until melted. Cool to room temperature. Beat whipping cream in large bowl until stiff peaks form. Fold cooled chocolate mixture into whipped cream. Refrigerate until of spreading consistency.

3. To assemble, split cake horizontally into 3 even layers. Place 1 cake layer on serving plate. Spread with one-fourth of frosting. Repeat with second layer. Top with third layer. Frost side and top with remaining frosting. Refrigerate.

4. For drizzle, place semisweet chocolate chips and shortening in 1-cup glass measuring cup. Microwave at MEDIUM (50% power) for 1 minute. Stir until smooth. Drizzle melted chocolate around outer top edge of cake, allowing mixture to run down side unevenly. Refrigerate until ready to serve. *Makes 12 to 16 servings*

Trifle Spectacular

1 package Duncan Hines® Moist Deluxe® Devil's Food Cake Mix

1 can (14 ounces) sweetened condensed milk

1 cup cold water

1 package (4-serving size) vanilla-flavor instant pudding and pie
   filling mix

2 cups whipping cream, whipped

2 tablespoons orange juice, divided

2¹/₂ cups sliced fresh strawberries, divided

1 pint fresh raspberries, divided

2 kiwifruit, peeled and sliced, divided

1¹/₂ cups frozen whipped topping, thawed for garnish

Mint leaves for garnish (optional)

1. Preheat oven to 350°F. Grease and flour two 9-inch round cake pans.

2. Prepare, bake and cool cake following package directions for original recipe. Cut one cake layer into 1-inch cubes. Freeze other cake layer for later use.

3. Combine sweetened condensed milk and water in large bowl. Stir until blended. Add pudding mix. Beat until thoroughly blended. Chill 5 minutes. Fold whipped cream into pudding mixture.

4. To assemble, spread 2 cups pudding mixture into 3-quart trifle dish (or 3-quart clear glass bowl with straight sides). Arrange half the cake cubes over pudding mixture. Sprinkle with 1 tablespoon orange juice. Layer with 1 cup strawberry slices, half the raspberries and one-third of kiwifruit slices. Repeat layers. Top with remaining pudding mixture. Garnish with whipped topping, remaining ¹/₂ cup strawberry slices, kiwifruit slices and mint leaves, if desired. *Makes 10 to 12 servings*

Chocolate Toffee Cream Cake

1 package DUNCAN HINES® Moist Deluxe® Dark Chocolate
    Fudge Cake Mix

3 eggs

1 $^1/_3$ cups water

$^1/_2$ cup vegetable oil

1 package (6 ounces) milk chocolate English toffee bits, divided

1 container (12 ounces) extra creamy non-dairy whipped topping,
    thawed

1. Preheat oven to 350°F. Grease and flour two 9-inch round cake pans.

2. Blend cake mix, eggs, water and oil in large mixing bowl until
moistened. Beat at medium speed with electric mixer for 4 minutes. Pour
into prepared pans. Bake at 350°F for 30 to 33 minutes or until
toothpick inserted in center comes out clean. Cool in pans 15 minutes.

3. Remove from pans. Cool completely. Reserve $^1/_4$ cup toffee bits; fold
remaining bits into whipped topping. Place one cake layer on serving
plate; spread with $^3/_4$ cup topping mixture. Top with remaining layer. Frost
sides and top with remaining topping mixture; garnish with reserved bits.
Refrigerate until ready to serve. *Makes 12 to 16 servings*

Tip: If chocolate toffee bits are not available, 4 chocolate covered toffee
candy bars can be substituted. Chop bars in a food processor until small
pieces form.

Chocolate Toffee Cream Cake

Easy Cream Cake

    1 package DUNCAN HINES® Moist Deluxe® Classic White
        Cake Mix
    3 egg whites
1 ⅓ cups half-and-half
    2 tablespoons vegetable oil
    1 cup flaked coconut, finely chopped
    ½ cup finely chopped pecans
    2 containers DUNCAN HINES® Creamy Home-Style Cream
        Cheese Frosting

1. Preheat oven to 350°F. Grease and flour three 8-inch round
cake pans.

2. Combine cake mix, egg whites, half-and-half, oil, coconut and pecans
in large bowl. Beat at low speed with electric mixer until moistened. Beat
at medium speed 2 minutes. Pour into prepared pans. Bake at 350°F for
22 to 25 minutes or until toothpick inserted in center comes out clean.
Cool following package directions.

3. To assemble, place one cake layer on serving plate. Spread with ¾ cup
Cream Cheese frosting. Place second cake layer on top. Spread with
¾ cup frosting. Top with third layer. Spread ¾ cup frosting on top only.
Garnish as desired.   *Makes 12 to 16 servings*

Tip: Spread leftover frosting between graham crackers for an easy and
delicious snack.

Easy Cream Cake

Pears en Croûte (Baked Pears in Pastry)

2 teaspoons granulated sugar

1/4 teaspoon ground cinnamon

1 egg white, lightly beaten

Cold water

1/4 cup golden raisins

1/4 cup chopped walnuts

2 tablespoons brown sugar

1 package DUNCAN HINES® Bakery-Style Cinnamon Muffin Mix

8 small ripe pears

1 cup all-purpose flour

1/2 cup shortening plus additional for greasing

Cinnamon sticks or vanilla beans, for garnish

Caramel flavor topping, at room temperature or warmed

1. Preheat oven to 375°F. Grease 13×9×2-inch pan.

2. Combine granulated sugar and cinnamon in small bowl; set aside. Combine beaten egg white and 1 teaspoon water in small bowl; set aside.

3. Combine raisins, walnuts, brown sugar, cinnamon swirl packet from Mix and cinnamon topping packet from Mix in medium bowl; set aside.

4. Core and peel pears; set aside.

5. Combine cinnamon muffin mix and flour in medium bowl. Cut in 1/2 cup shortening with pastry blender or 2 knives until flour is blended to form pea-size chunks. Sprinkle 5 tablespoons cold water, 1 tablespoon at a time, over flour mixture. Toss lightly with fork until dough forms ball.

6. Divide in half. Wrap one-half with plastic wrap; reserve. Roll remaining dough on well-floured surface to form 13-inch square. Cut square equally into four 6½-inch squares. Repeat using reserved dough ball.

7. To assemble, fill pear centers with 1½ tablespoons raisin mixture. Cover each pear with square of pastry. Mold with palm of hand to shape, folding corners under pear bottom. Place ¾ inch apart in prepared pan. Brush with egg white mixture. Sprinkle ¼ teaspoon cinnamon-sugar mixture over each pear.

8. Bake at 375°F for 33 to 35 minutes or until golden brown and pears are tender. Cool in pan for 5 minutes. Remove to serving dish. Insert cinnamon stick or piece of vanilla bean on top of pear to form stem. Drizzle caramel topping over pear, as desired. Serve warm or at room temperature. Refrigerate leftovers. *Makes 8 servings*

Note: To ripen pears, place in brown paper bag and store at room temperature for 24 to 48 hours.

Tip: Reroll leftover pastry. Cut into small leaf shapes. Place on baking sheet. Bake at 375°F for 8 to 10 minutes. Use as garnish.

Rich Pumpkin Cheesecake

CRUST

    1 package DUNCAN HINES® Moist Deluxe® Spice Cake Mix

    $^1/_2$ cup butter or margarine, melted

FILLING

    3 packages (8 ounces each) cream cheese, softened

    1 can (14 ounces) sweetened condensed milk

    1 can (16 ounces) solid pack pumpkin

    4 eggs

    1 tablespoon pumpkin pie spice

TOPPING

    1 package ($2^1/_2$ ounces) sliced almonds

    2 cups whipping cream, chilled

    $^1/_4$ cup sugar

1. Preheat oven to 375°F.

2. For crust, combine cake mix and melted butter in large bowl; press into bottom of *ungreased* 10-inch springform pan.

3. For filling, combine cream cheese and sweetened condensed milk in large bowl. Beat with electric mixer at high speed 2 minutes. Add pumpkin, eggs and pumpkin pie spice. Beat at high speed 1 minute. Pour over prepared crust in pan. Bake at 375°F for 65 to 70 minutes or until set. Cool completely on rack. Refrigerate 2 hours. Loosen cake from sides of pan; remove sides of pan.

4. For topping, preheat oven to 300°F. Toast almonds on baking sheet at 300°F for 4 to 5 minutes or until fragrant and light golden brown. Cool completely. Beat whipping cream in medium bowl with electric mixer on

high speed until soft peaks form. Gradually add sugar; beat until stiff peaks form. Spread over top of chilled cake. Garnish with toasted almonds. Refrigerate until ready to serve.   *Makes 8 to 12 servings*

Tip: To prepare in 13×9×2-inch pan, bake at 350°F 35 minutes or until set.

Rich Pumpkin Cheesecake

Della Robbia Cake

1 package DUNCAN HINES® Angel Food Cake Mix

1 1/2 teaspoons grated lemon peel

1 cup water

6 tablespoons granulated sugar

1 1/2 tablespoons cornstarch

1 tablespoon lemon juice

1/2 teaspoon vanilla extract

Few drops red food coloring

6 cling peach slices

6 medium strawberries, sliced

1. Preheat oven to 375°F.

2. Prepare cake mix as directed on package, adding lemon peel. Bake and cool cake as directed on package.

3. Combine water, sugar and cornstarch in small saucepan. Cook on medium-high heat until mixture thickens and clears. Remove from heat. Stir in lemon juice, vanilla extract and food coloring.

4. Alternate peach slices with strawberry slices around top of cake. Pour glaze over fruit and top of cake.   *Makes 12 to 16 servings*

Tip: For angel food cakes, always use a totally grease-free cake pan to get the best volume.

Della Robbia Cake

Children's Choice

Tell the kids you're making Chocolate
Chip Waffles or Brownie Ice Cream
Pie and watch their eyes light up.
When you start with Duncan Hines®
mixes kid-pleasing treats are almost as
much fun to make as they are to eat.

Berry Surprise Cupcakes

1 package DUNCAN HINES® Moist Deluxe® White Cake Mix
3 egg whites
1 1/3 cups water
2 tablespoons vegetable oil
3 sheets (0.5 ounce each) strawberry chewy fruit snacks
1 container DUNCAN HINES® Vanilla Frosting
2 pouches (0.9 ounce each) chewy fruit snack shapes, for garnish (optional)

1. Preheat oven to 350°F. Place 24 (2½-inch) paper liners in muffin cups.

2. Combine cake mix, egg whites, water and oil in large bowl. Beat at low speed with electric mixer until moistened. Beat at medium speed 2 minutes. Fill each liner half full with batter.

3. Cut three fruit snack sheets into 9 equal pieces. (You will have 3 extra squares.) Place each fruit snack piece on top of batter in each cup. Pour remaining batter equally over each. Bake at 350°F for 18 to 23 minutes or until toothpick inserted in center comes out clean. Cool in pans 5 minutes. Remove to cooling racks. Cool completely. Frost cupcakes with Vanilla frosting. Decorate with fruit snack shapes, if desired.

Makes 12 to 16 servings

Spring Break Blueberry Coffeecake

TOPPING

   1/2 cup flaked coconut

   1/4 cup firmly packed brown sugar

   2 tablespoons butter or margarine, softened

   1 tablespoon all-purpose flour

CAKE

   1 package DUNCAN HINES® Bakery-Style Wild Maine
      Blueberry Muffin Mix

   1 can (8 ounces) crushed pineapple with juice, undrained

   1 egg

   1/4 cup water

1. Preheat oven to 350°F. Grease 9-inch square pan.

2. For topping, combine coconut, brown sugar, butter and flour in small bowl. Mix with fork until well blended. Set aside.

3. Rinse blueberries from Mix with cold water and drain.

4. For cake, place muffin mix in medium bowl. Break up any lumps. Add pineapple with juice, egg and water. Stir until moistened, about 50 strokes. Fold in blueberries. Spread in pan. Sprinkle reserved topping over batter. Bake at 350°F for 30 to 35 minutes or until toothpick inserted into center comes out clean. Serve warm, or cool completely.

Makes 9 servings

Tip: To keep blueberries from discoloring the batter, drain them on paper towels after rinsing.

Chocolate Bunny Cookies

1 (21-ounce) package DUNCAN HINES® Family-Style Chewy
    Fudge Brownie Mix
1 egg
$^{1}/_{4}$ cup water
$^{1}/_{4}$ cup vegetable oil
1 $^{1}/_{3}$ cups pecan halves (96 halves)
1 container DUNCAN HINES® Creamy Home-Style Dark
    Chocolate Fudge Frosting
White chocolate chips

1. Preheat oven to 350°F. Grease baking sheets.

2. Combine brownie mix, egg, water and oil in large bowl. Stir with spoon until well blended, about 50 strokes. Drop by level tablespoonfuls 2 inches apart on greased baking sheets. Place two pecan halves, flat-side up, on each cookie for ears. Bake at 350°F for 10 to 12 minutes or until set. Cool 2 minutes on baking sheets. Remove to cooling racks. Cool completely.

3. Spread Dark Chocolate Fudge Frosting on one cookie. Place white chocolate chips, upside down, on frosting for eyes and nose. Dot each eye with frosting using toothpick. Repeat for remaining cookies. Allow frosting to set before storing cookies between layers of waxed paper in airtight container. *Makes 4 dozen cookies*

Tip: For variety, frost cookies with Duncan Hines® Vanilla Frosting and use semisweet chocolate chips for the eyes and noses.

Banana Split Cake

1 package DUNCAN HINES® Moist Deluxe® Banana Supreme
   Cake Mix

3 eggs

1 1/3 cups water

1/2 cup all-purpose flour

1/3 cup vegetable oil

1 cup mini semisweet chocolate chips

2 to 3 bananas

1 can (16 ounces) chocolate syrup

1 container (8 ounces) frozen whipped topping, thawed

1/2 cup chopped walnuts

   Colored sprinkles

   Maraschino cherries with stems, for garnish

1. Preheat oven to 350°F. Grease and flour 13×9×2-inch pan.

2. Combine cake mix, eggs, water, flour and oil in large bowl. Beat at low speed with electric mixer until moistened. Beat at medium speed 2 minutes. Stir in chocolate chips. Pour into prepared pan. Bake at 350°F for 32 to 35 minutes or until toothpick inserted in center comes out clean. Cool completely.

3. Slice bananas. Cut cake into squares; top with banana slices. Drizzle with chocolate syrup. Top with whipped topping, walnuts and sprinkles. Garnish with maraschino cherries.   *Makes 12 to 16 servings*

Tip: Dip bananas in diluted lemon juice to prevent darkening.

Banana Split Cake

Chocolate Chip Waffles

1 package DUNCAN HINES® Chocolate Chip Muffin Mix

3/4 cup all-purpose flour

1 teaspoon baking powder

1 3/4 cups milk

2 eggs

5 tablespoons butter or margarine, melted

Confectioners' sugar (optional)

1. Preheat and lightly grease waffle iron according to manufacturer's directions.

2. Combine muffin mix, flour and baking powder in large bowl. Add milk, eggs and melted butter. Stir until moistened, about 50 strokes. Pour batter onto center grids of preheated waffle iron. Bake according to manufacturer's directions until golden brown. Remove baked waffle carefully with fork. Repeat with remaining batter. Dust lightly with confectioners' sugar, if desired. Top with fresh fruit, syrup, grated chocolate or whipped cream, if desired.   *Makes 10 to 12 waffles*

Ice Cream Cookie Sandwich

2 pints chocolate chip ice cream, softened

1 package DUNCAN HINES® Moist Deluxe® Dark Chocolate
    Fudge Cake Mix

1/2 cup butter or margarine, softened

1. Line bottom of one 9-inch round cake pan with aluminum foil. Spread ice cream in pan; return to freezer until firm. Run knife around edge of pan to loosen ice cream. Remove from pan; wrap in foil and return to freezer.

2. Preheat oven to 350°F. Line bottom of two 9-inch round cake pans with aluminum foil. Place cake mix in large bowl. Add butter; mix thoroughly until crumbs form. Place half the cake mix in each prepared pan; press lightly. Bake at 350°F for 15 minutes or until browned around edges; do not overbake. Cool 10 minutes; remove from pans. Remove foil from cookie layers; cool completely.

3. To assemble, place one cookie layer on serving plate. Top with ice cream. Peel off foil. Place second cookie layer on top. Wrap in foil and freeze 2 hours. To keep longer, store in airtight container. Let stand at room temperature for 5 to 10 minutes before cutting.

Makes 10 to 12 servings

Ice Cream Cookie Sandwich

Take-Along Cake

1 package DUNCAN HINES® Moist Deluxe® Swiss Chocolate
   Cake Mix
1 package (12 ounces) semisweet chocolate chips
1 cup miniature marshmallows
1/4 cup butter or margarine, melted
1/2 cup packed brown sugar
1/2 cup chopped pecans or walnuts

1. Preheat oven to 350°F. Grease and flour 13×9-inch pan.

2. Prepare cake mix as directed on package. Add chocolate chips and marshmallows to batter. Pour into prepared pan. Drizzle melted butter over batter. Sprinkle with sugar and top with pecans. Bake at 350°F for 45 to 55 minutes or until toothpick inserted in center comes out clean. Serve warm or cool completely in pan.   *Makes 12 to 16 servings*

Tip: To keep leftover pecans fresh, store them in the freezer in an airtight container.

Take-Along Cake

Ice Cream Cone Cakes

1 package DUNCAN HINES® Moist Deluxe® Cake Mix (any flavor)

1 container DUNCAN HINES® Creamy Home-Style Chocolate Frosting

1 container DUNCAN HINES® Creamy Home-Style Vanilla Frosting

Chocolate sprinkles

Assorted decors

Jelly beans

2 maraschino cherries, for garnish

1. Preheat oven to 350°F. Grease and flour one 8-inch round cake pan and one 8-inch square pan.

2. Prepare cake following package directions for basic recipe. Pour about 2 cups batter into round pan. Pour about 3 cups batter into square pan. Bake at 350°F for 30 to 35 minutes or until toothpick inserted in center comes out clean. Cool following package directions.

3. To assemble, cut cooled cake and arrange as shown. Frost "cone" with Chocolate frosting, reserving ½ cup. Place writing tip in pastry bag. Fill with remaining ½ cup Chocolate frosting. Pipe waffle pattern onto "cones." Decorate with chocolate sprinkles. Spread Vanilla frosting on "ice cream." Decorate with assorted decors and jelly beans. Top each with maraschino cherry.   *12 to 16 servings*

Tip: Use tip of knife to draw lines in frosting for waffle pattern as guide for piping chocolate frosting.

Ice Cream Cone Cakes

Kids' Confetti Cake

CAKE

    1 package DUNCAN HINES® Moist Deluxe® Classic Yellow Cake
       Mix

    1 package (4-serving size) vanilla-flavor instant pudding and pie
       filling mix

    4 eggs

    1 cup water

    1/2 cup vegetable oil

    1 cup mini semisweet chocolate chips

TOPPING

    1 cup colored miniature marshmallows

    2/3 cup DUNCAN HINES® Creamy Home-Style Chocolate
       Frosting

    2 tablespoons mini semisweet chocolate chips

1. Preheat oven to 350°F. Grease and flour 13×9×2-inch baking pan.

2. For cake, combine cake mix, pudding mix, eggs, water and oil in large bowl. Beat at medium speed with electric mixer 2 minutes. Stir in 1 cup chocolate chips. Pour into prepared pan. Bake at 350°F for 40 to 45 minutes or until toothpick inserted in center comes out clean.

3. For topping, immediately arrange marshmallows evenly over hot cake. Place frosting in microwave-safe bowl. Microwave at HIGH (100% power) 25 to 30 seconds. Stir until smooth. Drizzle evenly over marshmallows and cake. Sprinkle with 2 tablespoons chocolate chips. Cool completely.   *Makes 12 to 16 servings*

Kids' Confetti Cake

Captivating Caterpillar Cupcakes

    1 package DUNCAN HINES® Moist Deluxe® White Cake Mix
    3 egg whites
1 ⅓ cups water
    2 tablespoons vegetable oil
 ½ cup star decors, divided
    1 container DUNCAN HINES® Vanilla Frosting
      Green food coloring
    6 chocolate sandwich cookies, finely crushed
 ½ cup candy-coated chocolate pieces
 ⅓ cup assorted jelly beans
      Assorted nonpareil decors

1. Preheat oven to 350°F. Place 24 (2½-inch) paper liners in muffin cups.

2. Combine cake mix, egg whites, water and oil in large bowl. Beat at low speed with electric mixer until moistened. Beat at medium speed 2 minutes. Fold in ⅓ cup star decors. Fill paper liners about half full. Bake at 350°F for 18 to 23 minutes or until toothpick inserted in center comes out clean. Cool in pans 5 minutes. Remove to cooling racks. Cool completely.

3. Tint vanilla frosting with green food coloring. Frost one cupcake. Sprinkle ½ teaspoon chocolate cookie crumbs on frosting. Arrange 4 candy-coated chocolate pieces to form caterpillar body. Place jelly bean at one end to form head. Attach remaining star and nonpareil decors with dots of frosting to form eyes. Repeat with remaining cupcakes.

Makes 24 cupcakes

Captivating Caterpillar Cupcakes

Hot Fudge Sundae Cake

1 package DUNCAN HINES® Moist Deluxe® Dark Chocolate
    Fudge Cake Mix
1/2 gallon brick vanilla ice cream

FUDGE SAUCE
  1 can (12 ounces) evaporated milk
1 1/4 cups sugar
  4 squares (1 ounce each) unsweetened chocolate
  1/4 cup butter or margarine
1 1/2 teaspoons vanilla extract
  1/4 teaspoon salt
    Whipped cream and maraschino cherries for garnish

1. Preheat oven to 350°F. Grease and flour 13×9×2-inch pan. Prepare, bake and cool cake following package directions.

2. Remove cake from pan. Split cake in half horizontally. Place bottom layer back in pan. Cut ice cream into even slices and place evenly over bottom cake layer (use all the ice cream). Place remaining cake layer over ice cream. Cover and freeze.

3. For fudge sauce, combine evaporated milk and sugar in medium saucepan. Stir constantly on medium heat until mixture comes to a rolling boil. Boil and stir for 1 minute. Add unsweetened chocolate and stir until melted. Beat over medium heat until smooth. Remove from heat. Stir in butter, vanilla extract and salt.

4. Cut cake into serving squares. For each serving, place cake square on plate; spoon hot fudge sauce on top. Garnish with whipped cream and maraschino cherry. *Makes 12 to 16 servings*

Hot Fudge Sundae Cake

Turtle Cake

1 package DUNCAN HINES® Moist Deluxe® Fudge Marble
    Cake Mix
6 fun-size chocolate-covered nougat, caramel, peanut candy bars
1 container (16 ounces) DUNCAN HINES® Creamy Home-Style
    Cream Cheese Frosting, divided
    Green food coloring
2 tablespoons sliced almonds
    Candy-coated chocolate pieces
    White chocolate chips

1. Preheat oven to 350°F. Grease and flour 2½-quart ovenproof glass bowl with rounded bottom.

2. Prepare cake following package directions for original recipe. Pour into prepared bowl. Bake at 350°F for 55 to 60 minutes or until toothpick inserted in center comes out clean. Cool in bowl 20 minutes. Invert onto cooling rack. Cool completely.

3. Place cake on serving plate. Remove 1-inch cake square from upper side of cake for head. Insert 2 fun-size candy bars, flat sides together, into square hole for head. Position remaining 4 candy bars under cake for feet. Reserve 1 teaspoon Cream Cheese frosting. Tint remaining Cream Cheese frosting with green food coloring; frost cake. Sprinkle almonds on top. Place candy-coated chocolate pieces around bottom edge of shell. Attach white chocolate chips to head with reserved frosting for eyes.

Makes 12 to 16 servings

Turtle Cake

Quick Rocky Road Cake

1 package DUNCAN HINES® Moist Deluxe® Devil's Food
    Cake Mix
1 container DUNCAN HINES® Creamy Home-Style Classic
    Vanilla Frosting
$1/2$ cup creamy peanut butter
$1/3$ cup semi-sweet chocolate chips
$1/3$ cup salted cocktail peanuts

1. Preheat oven to 350°F. Grease and flour 13×9×2-inch pan.

2. Prepare, bake and cool cake following package directions for basic recipe.

3. Combine Vanilla Frosting and peanut butter in medium bowl. Frost top of cake. Sprinkle with chocolate chips and peanuts.

Makes 12 to 16 servings

Tip: For an easy treat for kids, follow package directions for making cupcakes. Frost and decorate as directed above.

Brownie Ice Cream Pie

1 (21-ounce) package DUNCAN HINES® Chewy Fudge
    Brownie Mix
2 eggs
$1/2$ cup vegetable oil
$1/4$ cup water
$3/4$ cup semisweet chocolate chips
1 (9-inch) unbaked pastry crust
1 (10-ounce) package frozen sweetened sliced strawberries
    Vanilla ice cream

1. Preheat oven to 350°F.

2. Combine brownie mix, eggs, oil and water in large bowl. Stir with spoon until well blended, about 50 strokes. Stir in chocolate chips. Spoon into crust. Bake at 350°F for 40 to 45 minutes or until set. Cool completely. Purée strawberries in food processor or blender. Cut pie into wedges. Serve with ice cream and puréed strawberries.   *Makes 8 servings*

Brownie Ice Cream Pie

Marshmallow Krispie Bars

1 (21-ounce) package DUNCAN HINES® Family-Style Chewy
    Fudge Brownie Mix
1 package (10$\frac{1}{2}$ ounces) miniature marshmallows
1$\frac{1}{2}$ cups semisweet chocolate chips
1 cup creamy peanut butter
1 tablespoon butter or margarine
1$\frac{1}{2}$ cups crisp rice cereal

1. Preheat oven to 350°F. Grease bottom only of 13×9-inch pan.

2. Prepare and bake brownies following package directions for cake-like recipe. Remove from oven. Sprinkle marshmallows on hot brownies. Return to oven. Bake for 3 minutes longer.

3. Place chocolate chips, peanut butter and butter in medium saucepan. Cook over low heat, stirring constantly, until chips are melted. Add rice cereal; mix well. Spread mixture over marshmallow layer. Refrigerate until chilled. Cut into bars. *Makes about 2 dozen bars*

Tip: For a special presentation, cut cookies into diamond shapes.

VOLUME MEASUREMENTS (dry)

$^1/_8$ teaspoon = 0.5 mL
$^1/_4$ teaspoon = 1 mL
$^1/_2$ teaspoon = 2 mL
$^3/_4$ teaspoon = 4 mL
1 teaspoon = 5 mL
1 tablespoon = 15 mL
2 tablespoons = 30 mL
$^1/_4$ cup = 60 mL
$^1/_3$ cup = 75 mL
$^1/_2$ cup = 125 mL
$^2/_3$ cup = 150 mL
$^3/_4$ cup = 175 mL
1 cup = 250 mL
2 cups = 1 pint = 500 mL
3 cups = 750 mL
4 cups = 1 quart = 1 L

VOLUME MEASUREMENTS (fluid)

1 fluid ounce (2 tablespoons) = 30 mL
4 fluid ounces ($^1/_2$ cup) = 125 mL
8 fluid ounces (1 cup) = 250 mL
12 fluid ounces (1$^1/_2$ cups) = 375 mL
16 fluid ounces (2 cups) = 500 mL

WEIGHTS (mass)

$^1/_2$ ounce = 15 g
1 ounce = 30 g
3 ounces = 90 g
4 ounces = 120 g
8 ounces = 225 g
10 ounces = 285 g
12 ounces = 360 g
16 ounces = 1 pound = 450 g

DIMENSIONS

$^1/_{16}$ inch = 2 mm
$^1/_8$ inch = 3 mm
$^1/_4$ inch = 6 mm
$^1/_2$ inch = 1.5 cm
$^3/_4$ inch = 2 cm
1 inch = 2.5 cm

OVEN TEMPERATURES

250°F = 120°C
275°F = 140°C
300°F = 150°C
325°F = 160°C
350°F = 180°C
375°F = 190°C
400°F = 200°C
425°F = 220°C
450°F = 230°C

BAKING PAN SIZES

Utensil	Size in Inches/Quarts	Metric Volume	Size in Centimeters
Baking or Cake Pan (square or rectangular)	8×8×2	2 L	20×20×5
	9×9×2	2.5 L	23×23×5
	12×8×2	3 L	30×20×5
	13×9×2	3.5 L	33×23×5
Loaf Pan	8×4×3	1.5 L	20×10×7
	9×5×3	2 L	23×13×7
Round Layer Cake Pan	8×1½	1.2 L	20×4
	9×1½	1.5 L	23×4
Pie Plate	8×1¼	750 mL	20×3
	9×1¼	1 L	23×3
Baking Dish or Casserole	1 quart	1 L	—
	1½ quart	1.5 L	—
	2 quart	2 L	—